Presentation Skills

90 Minute Guides

Michelle N. Halsey

Copyright © 2016 Silver City Publications & Training, L.L.C.

Silver City Publications & Training, L.L.C.
P.O. Box 1914
Nampa, ID 83653
https://www.silvercitypublications.com/shop/

ISBN-10: 1-64004-033-1
ISBN-13: 978-1-64004-033-5

Contents

Chapter 1 – Creating the Program

We will look at the beginning steps to follow when creating a plan to improve your Presentation Skills. The first thing to look at is to perform a Needs Analysis. This will help you to understand your audience and provide you with the answers to a few basic questions. A basic outline and some minor research would then be utilized to help create the basic program that will assist you in developing greater Presentation Skills.

Performing a Needs Analysis

A needs analysis measures what skills employees have -- and what they need. It indicates how to deliver the right training at the right time. The results answer the following questions:

- What is the **audience** with the problem or need for change?

- What **tasks** and subtasks does an expert perform to complete a work process?

- What **gaps** exist between experts, average, and poor performers of a work process?

- How do we translate the needs into objectives to promote a strong learning **outcome**?

The method can be simple; observation, careful note taking, and asking questions work.

Question	Methods
Audience?	Interview key stakeholders and listen to their concerns about the problem.
	Define who needs help to overcome the problem.
	Identify and describe the audience and the work.

Tasks?	Observe the work being done by recognized experts.
	Take careful notes and ask questions where needed.
	Document the proper performance of the work tasks.
Gaps?	Observe other workers doing the tasks.
	Compare results with the performance of experts. Document identified skill gaps.
Outcome?	Develop a complete list of tasks for performing the work completely and correctly.

Example: Although the call center reps are empowered to assist customers, several are not solving callers' product problems. Instead, they are passing them on to the Escalation Desk, creating a bottleneck -- and unhappy customers. The needs analysis identified a task called "Resolve customer complaints". Some of its subtasks are:

- Answer call

- Listen to customer's problem

- Express empathy for the trouble

- Open a new support ticket

- Resolve complaint per the list of allowable resolutions

- Document resolution in the call notes

- Close support ticket.

Writing the Basic Outline

To develop the outline, group the tasks that fit together logically, and create headings that reflect the goal of the subtasks.

Handling a Call

- Answer call

- Listen to customer's problem

- Express empathy for the trouble

- Open a new support ticket

- Resolve the complaint per the list of allowable resolutions

Documenting Call Resolution

- Document the resolution in the call notes

- Close support ticket

Add headings for an introduction and workshop objectives at the beginning -- and a wrap-up and evaluation at the end, and your basic outline is complete.

Researching, Writing, and Editing

Researching: The needs analysis has likely produced much of the supporting content required to build the program. However, if information gaps exist, return to your expert performers (also termed subject matter experts) and ask questions.

Writing: If you're using a word processor, create a template so your material is consistent from the beginning. Assign a preliminary time length to each module based on the total time available for the presentation. (You'll validate it later.) When writing, aim for brevity. The more you say, the less the audience remembers.

Make sure to validate your finalized content before you move on to editing.

Editing: As you edit, write for the ear, not for the eyes. Make sure sentences are twenty words or less and only convey one thought. Use simple, familiar words. Make sure that you have provided the definitions of any terms important to the learning experience. Try to spice up your module titles.

Chapter 2 – Choosing Your Delivery Methods

Now it's time to determine what methods you will use to deliver your presentation. We will be beginning by covering basic delivery methods. Once we have a good foundation and grasp on the basic methods we will delve into more advanced methods.

Basic Methods

Lecture: If you must lecture occasionally, use strategies to make the delivery more interactive.

Discussion: A discussion facilitated by the presenter can be rich in interactivity.

Small Group learning experiences: A small group experience provides direction toward specific learning goals, and provides a high degree of participant involvement.

- **Dyads (Groups of 2).** Using pairs provides unlimited options for simple interactive experiences. You can say, "Turn to the person on your right and…" Using dyads manages the attention span, the extent of influence, and the focus of the goal. The learning experience is relatively intimate.

- **Triads (Groups of 3).** Trios expand the focus and experience opportunities. A measure of intimacy is still retained, but multiple viewpoints can be contributed. Triads are useful for producing definitions, establishing priorities, or providing an ongoing support system.

Case Study: The case study method is the presentation of detailed information about a particular situation, often problem solving. Case studies can be very creative exercises, and they are well-suited for small groups. Here are six guidelines for developing a case study:

1. Determine the principle you wish to have the case emphasize

2. Establish a situation that demonstrates the principle

3. Develop appropriate symptoms

4. Develop the characters

5. Write the case

6. Provide questions to guide the learners as they process the case study to solve a problem.

Advanced Methods

After you feel comfortable with basic delivery methods, you can begin to explore some of the more challenging ways to present and facilitate learning experiences.

Role play: Role playing allows participants to act out a behavioral role. This exercise -- done with small groups or the large group -- allows members to expand their awareness of varying points of view, and provides an experiential learning opportunity. A role play can be used in several ways; to solve a participant problem, clarify or sharpen an issue, or demonstrate a skill approach to a task. Importantly, it gives people an opportunity to practice a skill or approach in a safe environment and use the experience later on the job.

Here are several tips for managing a role play exercises:

• Obtain volunteers, rather than making assignments

• Use role play later in the training session, when participants know each other better

• Select low-threat situations, such as a work group holding a staff meeting.

Problem solving: Problem solving experiences are increasingly popular in training presentations because they allow participants to gain "real world" experience that often provides direct transfer back to the job.

There are three phases to a problem solving exercise:

1. Defining the problem and generating data about it

2. Generating potential solutions

3. Selecting an implementing a solution.

Below are several of the many proven methods that are available to help participants with each phase.

Phase	Method	Description
Defining the problem and generating data about it	Pareto Analysis	Vilfredo Pareto, a mathematician and economist coined the "80/20" rule. A Pareto Analysis allows you to group and analyze data for a problem such as defects in a model of kitchen faucet.
	Force Field Analysis	Kurt Lewin defined driving forces and restraining forces that influence the solution to a problem.
Generating potential solutions	Brainstorming	Brainstorming allows a group to generate a large volume of ideas about a problem, or potential solutions. Later, the results must be condensed to a workable number of ideas, typically through grouping, and then voted on.
	The Delphi Technique	Originally used by the RAND corporation, the Delphi technique allows the anonymous generating of ideas which are then filtered.
Selecting and implementing a solution	Ranking	Participants rank options on a given scale, with or without criteria.
	The Journalist's Six Questions	Use "who, what, when, where, why and how" questions to generate data.

Basic Criteria to Consider

A training presentation may use any combination of delivery methods as long as the net result is to achieve learning outcomes -- and consider organizational requirements and constraints. The four-step process below will help you select the best training delivery options to meet your training needs.

1. List all possible learning methodologies that could be used to achieve the session objectives

2. Identify possible delivery options for the learning methodologies

3. Identify the organizational, presenter, facility, and resource parameters and their impact on the delivery options.

4. Recommend your delivery strategies.

At a bank, the outcome of the process might look like this:

Objective	Delivery Strategy	Expansion/Notes
List the five key customer support principles at the bank	Lecture only the principles, using the flip chart or PowerPoint for emphasis, and then add interactivity	Find a lead-off story Develop a group problem-solving exercise to provide follow-up practice
Demonstrate a performance problem with a customer support team in a bank	Role play	Use triads Find extra space
Generate ideas for improving customer support service	Brainstorming	Procure additional flip charts for groups

Chapter 3 – Verbal Communication Skills

Communication skills are needed to be able to provide an excellent presentation. Without being able to verbalize your ideas and opinions there is very little chance of having a successful presentation. We will begin by looking at listening and hearing skills, asking the correct questions and finish with communicating with more power.

Listening and Hearing: They Aren't the Same Thing

Hearing is the act of perceiving sound by the ear. Assuming an individual is not hearing-impaired, hearing simply happens. Listening, however, is something that one consciously chooses to do. Listening requires concentration so that the brain processes meaning from words and sentences. Listening leads to learning.

This is not always an easy task. The normal adult rate of speech is 100-150 words per minute, but the brain can think at a rate of 400-500 words per minute, leaving extra time for daydreaming, or anticipating the speaker's or the recipient's next words. Listening skills, however, can be learned and refined.

Asking Questions

Three types of questions are useful in a presentation; open questions, clarifying questions, and closed questions.

Open Questions: Open questions stimulate thinking and discussion or responses including opinions or feelings. They pass control of the conversation to the respondent. Leading words in open questions include: *Why, what, or how*. A statement such as *"describe the characteristics of the car"* is really an open question. Examples of open questions include:

- Describe the style of the leader of the meeting.

- How do you feel when you hit a home run?

Asking questions is both an art and a science. Your questions in a presentation should be:

- Clear and concise, covering a single issue

- Reasonable, based on what participants are expected to know

- Challenging, to provoke thought

- Honest and relevant, eliciting logical answers

Clarifying Questions: A clarifying question helps to remove ambiguity, elicits additional detail, and guides you as you answer a question. Below are some examples:

- You said you liked apples more than oranges, why is that?

- What sort of savings are you looking to achieve?

Closed Questions: Closed questions usually require a one-word answer, and shut off discussion. Closed questions provide facts, allow the questioner to maintain control of the conversation, and are easy to answer. Typical leading words are: *Is, can, how many, or does*. Below are several examples of closed questions:

- Who will lead the meeting?

- Do you know how to open the emergency exit door on this aircraft?

Phrasing: To evoke an answer, your question should use phrasing that is:

- *Clear and concise*, covering a single issue

- *Reasonable*, based on what participants are expected to know

- *Challenging*, to provoke thought

- *Honest and relevant*, directing participants to logical answers.

Directing Questions appropriately: Should you direct your questions to individuals or to an entire group? When you direct a question to an individual, you:

- Stimulate one participant to think and respond

- Tap the known resources of an "expert" in the room

If you choose to direct your question to the group instead, you:

- Stimulate the thinking of all participants

- Provide participants the opportunity to respond voluntarily

- Avoid putting any one person on the spot.

The following exercise provides practice with questioning concepts and techniques.

Communicating with Power

It's been said that you have between thirty seconds and two minutes to capture your participants' attention. It's critical to engage people from the beginning.

Voice: 38% of the message received by a listener is governed by the tone and quality of your voice. The pitch, volume, and control of your voice all make a difference in audience perception.

Characteristics	Description	Tips
Pitch	How high or low your voice is	Avoid a high-pitched sound. Speak from your stomach, the location of your diaphragm.
Volume	The loudness of your voice must be governed by your diaphragm	Speak through your diaphragm, not your throat
Quality	The color, warmth, and meaning given to your voice	Add emotion to your voice. Smile as much as possible when you are speaking

Command: Selecting a good opener is an important way to take command of an audience. Making judicious use of certain types of remarks will endear you to the audience from the moment the program starts.

- A dramatic story

- A reference to a current or well-known news story

- A personal experience

- A rhetorical question

- A historical event

- Adventure, either past or present.

More Tips

- Did we say practice? And practice again?

- Smile

- Stand up straight and tall

- Rivet your participants with eye contact

- Dress like your audience, or one level above it.

Chapter 4 – Non-Verbal Communication Skills

Understanding your body language and other physical cues is very important when you are presenting material in front of an audience. Your non-verbal communication skills are just as important as your verbal skills. Combined they make up the complete communication package that you use when you are presenting your material.

Body Language

Non-verbal communication is the process of communication through sending and receiving wordless messages. It is the single most powerful form of communication. Nonverbal communication cues you in to what is on another person's mind, even more than voice or words can do.

One study at UCLA found that up to 93 percent of communication effectiveness is determined by nonverbal cues. Another study indicated that the impact of a performance was determined 7 percent by the words used, 38 percent by voice quality, and 55 percent by non-verbal communication.

Body language is a form of non-verbal communication involving the use of stylized gestures, postures, and physiologic signs which act as cues to other people. Humans unconsciously send and receive non-verbal signals through body language all the time.

Your words represent only 7% of the message that is received. Your body language represents 55%. But your body language must match the words used. If a conflict arises between your words and your body language, your body language governs.

Gestures

Gestures are an important tool for a presenter. The challenge is to make gestures support the speaking, reinforcing ideas. Below are several basic rules for the use of gestures:

- Make most gestures above the waist. (Those below the waist suggest failure, defeat, and despair.)

- Hold your forearms parallel to the waist, with your elbows about 3 inches from the side.

- Make your hands part of your forearm, opening them, with your fingers slightly curved. (Limp hands may indicate a lack of leadership.)

- Use both hands to convey power.

Gestures of direction, size, shape, description, feeling, and intensity are all effective when speaking.

The Signals You Send to Others

Signals are movements used to communicate needs, desires, and feelings to others. They are a form of expressive communication. More than 75% of the signals you send to others are non-verbal.

People who are excellent communicators are sensitive to the power of the emotions and thoughts communicated non-verbally through signals.

Types of Non-Verbal Signals: Other than gestures already discussed, signals include:

- Eye contact

- Posture

- Body movements

They all convey important information that isn't put into words. By paying closer attention to other people's nonverbal behaviors, you will improve your own ability to communicate nonverbally.

Intervals of four to five seconds of eye contact are recommended.

It is also important to use a tone of voice to reinforce the words in your presentation. For example, using an animated tone of voice emphasizes your enthusiasm for a participant's contribution in a debrief session.

As a presenter, your words should match your non-verbal behaviors. If they do not, people will tend to pay less attention to what you said, and focus instead on your nonverbal signals.

It's Not What You Say, It's How You Say It

Tone of Voice: We are all born with a particular tone of voice. While most people are not gifted with a radio announcer's voice, we can learn to improve our tone of voice. The idea is have your voice sound upbeat, warm, under control, and clear. Here are some tips to help you begin the process.

- Make sure you are breathing from the diaphragm.

- Stay hydrated by drinking lots of water and avoid caffeine due to its diuretic effects

- Stand up tall; posture affects breathing, which affects tone.

- Smile; it warms up the tone of your voice.

- If your voice is particularly high or low, exercise the range of your voice by doing a sliding scale. You can also expand the range of your voice by singing.

- Record your voice and analyze the playback.

- Practice speaking in a slightly lower octave. Deeper voices have more credibility than higher pitched voices. It will take getting used to pitching your voice down an octave, but it will be worth the effort.

- Get feedback from a colleague or family member about the tone of your voice.

Chapter 5 – Overcoming Nervousness

Nervousness is normal when giving a presentation. After all, public speaking is the top fear in the top ten lists of fears. Nervousness can strike at different points in a presentation:

- At the beginning

- If you feel the audience has slipped away from you

- If your memory betrays you.

This module will provide you with concrete strategies for overcoming presentation jitters.

Preparing Mentally

Visualization is the formation of mental visual images. It is an excellent way to prepare your mind before a presentation. There are several types of visualization:

Receptive Visualization: Relax, clear your mind, sketch a vague scene, ask a question, and wait for a response. You might imagine you are on the beach, hearing and smelling the sea. You might ask, "Why can't I relax?", and the answer may flow into your consciousness.

Programmed Visualization: Create an image, giving it sight, taste, sound, and smell. Imagine a goal you want to reach, or a healing you wish to accelerate. Jane used visualization when she took up running, feeling the push of running the hills, the sweat, and the press to the finish line.

Guided Visualization: Visualize again a scene in detail, but this time leave out important elements. Wait for your subconscious to supply missing pieces to your puzzle. Your scene could be something pleasant from the past.

The process for Effective Visualization

- Loosen your clothing, sit or lie down in a quiet place, and close your eyes softly.

- Scan your body, seeking tension in specific muscles. Relax those muscles as much as you can.

- Form mental sense impressions. Involve all your senses; sight, hearing, smell, touch and taste.

- Use affirmations. Repeat short, positive statements and avoid negatives such as "I am not tense"; rather, say "I am letting go of tension."

- Use affirmations. Repeat short, positive statements that affirm your ability to relax now. Use present tense and positive language. As an example:

- Tension flows from my body

- I can relax at will.

- I am in harmony with life.

- Peace is within me.

Visualize three times a day. It's easiest if you visualize in the morning and at night while lying in bed. Soon, you will be able to visualize just about anywhere, especially before a presentation.

Physical Relaxation Techniques

People who are nervous tend to breathe many short, shallow breaths in their upper chest. Breathing exercises can alleviate this. You can do most breathing exercises anywhere. Below are some exercises that will assist you in relaxing.

Breathing Exercises: Deliberately controlling your breathing can help a person calm down. Ways to do this include: breathing through one's nose and exhaling through one's mouth, breathing from one's diagram, and breathing rhythmically.

Meditation: Meditation is a way of exercising mental discipline. Most meditation techniques involve increasing self-awareness, monitoring thoughts, and focusing. Meditation techniques include prayer, the repetition of a mantra, and relaxing movement or postures.

Progressive Muscle Relaxation (PMR): PMR is a technique of stress management that involves mentally inducing your muscles to tense and relax. PMR usually focuses on areas of the body where tension is commonly felt, such as the head, shoulders, and chest area. It's a way to exercise the power of the mind over the body.

Visualization: Visualization is the use of mental imagery to induce relaxation. Some visualization exercise involves picturing a place of serenity and comfort, such as a beach or a garden. Other visualization exercises involve imagining the release of anger in a metaphorical form. An example of this latter kind of visualization is imagining one's anger as a ball to be released to space.

Appearing Confident in Front of the Crowd

In addition to everything we've discussed, below are some tips for maintaining your confidence when you're "on".

- Get a good night's sleep

- Practice your words along with your visuals

- Have a full "dress rehearsal"

- If you are traveling to a new site out of town, try to arrive early in the evening and locate the site. That way you won't be frazzled in the morning, trying to locate the venue.

Chapter 6 – Creating Fantastic Flip Charts

Information written on flip charts enhances the learning process. During a presentation, the use of flip charts serves to inform participants, record information, and focus attention on a topic. They represent a simple, low-cost learning aid -- with no requirements for power or technology, and no worries about burned-out bulbs or darkened rooms. Flip charts add versatility to a presentation, and allow the presenter to use creativity to enhance the learning process.

Required Tools

At a minimum, you will need a flip chart easel, several pads of flip chart paper, a few sets of colored markers, and masking tape for posting the results of exercises. Also handy are several packages of sticky notes to flag specific pages, and a straight edge. You may want to plan to cover up information that you will reveal at a given time during the presentation and then have some pre-cut paper available, sized appropriately for the text.

If you are bringing pre-written charts to an off-site presentation, you will also need some type of container to protect the pages.

The Advantages of Pre-Writing

There are many good reasons to pre-write your flip chart content.

- **Confidence**: You are in control of the material for your presentation – design, organization, and appearance. This also helps reduce nervousness.

- **Appearance**: Your material has a specific "look and feel" that is not necessarily easy to achieve when prepared during a session.

- **Time**: With your charts ready ahead of the presentation, the time during a presentation is used for learning activities, not writing, which keeps your back to the participants.

Tips:

- Always print; never use handwriting

- Consider using a straight edge to stem tendency to write "downhill"

- If you are using charts in a sequence, number them.

Using Colors Appropriately

Good use of color can make the difference in the dynamics of a presentation -- and participants' acceptance of the content. Conversely, the effect of a great chart can suffer from the poor use of color. According to the Optical Society of America, blue, black, and green offer the greatest visibility, and blue is the most pleasing color. Avoid purple, brown, pink, and yellow for any type of general printing.

The use of two or three color combinations can be very effective. Here are several rules.

- Red and orange should only be used as accent colors for bullets, underlines, or arrows, or for key words when everything else is in black or blue

- Avoid orange and blue together

- Never use yellow.

When creating your charts, take some time to think about the colors you are using, and how they can enhance the understanding of your topic.

Creating a Plan B

Paper is not permanent, even if you are presenting at your own location. And if you're flying with your materials or shipping them, packages do occasionally get lost or damaged. You will need a backup plan in case something happens. Below are some tasks for creating your Plan B.

- Keep documents on your computer organized by course, reflecting the content and order sequence of each flip chart.

- Make paper handouts of the most critical information on the charts.

- Take pictures of the chart pages, and have the camera or images with you on site.

- If you have time to re-create some of your charts, enlist a volunteer to help you reconstruct the most critical ones.

- If you will be returning to the site, consider leaving a set of your charts with a trusted colleague until you return.

- As time permits, duplicate your charts in PowerPoint. Although you will probably continue to use flip charts, having them available in PowerPoint becomes a backup.

Chapter 7 – Creating Compelling PowerPoint Presentations

Microsoft PowerPoint is a commanding tool for creating visual screens for a presentation. Visuals created in PowerPoint and projected on a screen are often easier to see in a large room than information displayed on a flip chart. Using PowerPoint offers the following benefits:

- Allows you to add emphasis to important concepts, helping to increase retention of information

- Adds variety to your presentation

- Makes it easier to display images, charts, or graphs possibly too complex for a flip chart.

Also, PowerPoint files can easily be shared with participants or others after the session.

Required Tools

To create and use a Microsoft PowerPoint file to support your presentation outline, you will need:

- Microsoft Office PowerPoint software for Microsoft Windows or Macintosh OS

- A Windows or a MAC computer equipped with the minimum hardware and software specifications for your version of PowerPoint

- An LCD or DLP projector

- A projection screen

Optionally, you may wish to add the following to your toolkit:

- Storage media such as a USB memory stick or CD-R disc

- An extension cord

- A laser pointer for emphasis during the discussion of a PowerPoint slide.

Tips and Tricks

Use the following suggestions to enhance the benefit of your PowerPoint presentation.

Overall Appearance

- Display only one major concept on each slide

- Use short phrases or bullet points rather than paragraphs

- Limit each line of text to no more than 7-8 words

- Allow only 7-8 lines of text per slide

- Use images sparingly; one or two per slide

- Leave a good amount of blank space in your presentation

- Create a title for each slide

- Use effects, transitions animation, and sound very sparingly.

Fonts and Color

- Use simple sans serif fonts such as Helvetica or Arial for readability

- Select a point size of 32 or larger for titles, and 20 points for body text

- Use colors that work well together, such as yellow or white on a dark blue background.

- Check the readability and visibility of your fonts and color choices with the lighting in the room in which you will present.

Preparation

- Make sure to match your slides to the purpose of the presentation

- Develop a template and stick to it for a consistent look and feel

Computer

- Check your equipment, computer settings, and room lighting in advance

- Before your presentation, turn off screensavers, instant messaging, and email notifications

- Make sure that your computer's power management console will not automatically shut the system down after a set amount of time.

Creating a Plan B

While technology allows you to make great enhancements to a presentation, it also offers more opportunities for technical trouble. Here are some suggestions to keep your presentation moving along, even if the technology isn't.

- Make one or more backup copies of your PowerPoint file on the computer on which you plan to show the presentation.

- Before the presentation, download and install the free Microsoft PowerPoint Viewer available at www.microsoft.com. In the event that your PowerPoint software won't run, you will still be able to use the viewer to show your PowerPoint slides.

- Copy your PowerPoint file onto a USB Drive. That way, if you have a computer problem, you can move the file to another one, if available.

- Bring sufficient printed copies of your presentation for participants. If logistics prevent that, plan to have at least one copy available for photocopying on site.

- If all else fails, write your key points on a flip chart.

Chapter 8 – Wow Them with the Whiteboard

A whiteboard is the name for any glossy-surfaced writing board where non-permanent markings can be made. Unlike the predecessor chalkboard, there is no chalk dust, and markings remain longer than they would on a chalkboard.

Whiteboards have been around since the 1970's, and are now vastly improved and more affordable compared to early models. The use of a whiteboard helps to promote interactivity during a presentation.

Traditional and Electronic Whiteboards

Traditional Whiteboards: Traditional whiteboards are attached to the wall, or are available in free-standing frames. Unlike pre-written flip chart paper sheets, whiteboards cannot easily be moved from site to site. However, they are usually larger, and are useful for recording the results of small group exercises or spontaneous information arising in a discussion. Traditional whiteboards cost less than $100, or up to $1,000. A traditional whiteboard requires a set of wet or dry erase whiteboard markers, a whiteboard eraser, and whiteboard cleaning solution.

Electronic Whiteboards: An electronic whiteboard looks like a traditional whiteboard, but is a unique combination of hardware and software. The surface is connected to a computer and a projector. A projector beams the computer's desktop onto the board's surface, where users control the computer using a pen, finger, or other device. Uses include:

- Operating any software that is loaded onto the connected PC, including web browsers and proprietary software

- Using software to electronically capture text or marks written on the whiteboard

- Translating cursive writing to text

- Controlling the PC.

Because the markings on the whiteboard are digitized, the resulting electronic information can be stored, printed, or shared in real time with participants in other locations. Electronic whiteboards cost more than $1,000.

Using Colors Appropriately

Colors on a whiteboard are often more vivid than those on a flip chart. Otherwise, most of the same rules apply:

- Blue, black, and green offer the greatest visibility, with blue the most pleasing color.

- Avoid purple, brown, pink, and yellow for any type of general printing.

- The use of two or three color combinations can be very effective; however orange should only be used with red as an accent color. Never use yellow, and avoid orange and blue together.

Creating a Plan B

Traditional Whiteboards: When using a traditional whiteboard, have extra markers on hand, because they tend to dry up easily.

If your presentation is longer than one day, plan to make a backup of your work from the computer to a USB flash drive in the event that they are erased overnight.

Electronic Whiteboards: If you are working with an electronic whiteboard and encounter technical issues, you can show a previously created PowerPoint presentation through a projector. Plan to carry at least one copy of the PowerPoint handouts for duplication if needed. You can always quickly jot down key points on a flip chart.

Regardless of which type of whiteboard is used, key content should be available in a handout master or on flip chart pages as a backup.

Chapter 9 – Vibrant Videos and Amazing Audio

Audio and video are very much a part of our everyday lives, so they are accepted --and even expected media in a presentation. They are attractive options for a presentation because they provide learners with more dimensions by which to receive information. While video and audio both represent a one-way communication to participants, the opportunity to use them as part of learning exercises or in the ensuing discussions adds value to the presentation.

Video

There are three main ways to obtain video material:

- Creating your own media using a small personal video camera

- Purchasing off-the-shelf video designed for training presentations

- Hiring a professional video production company.

Your media budget, the amount of available preparation time, your comfort and skill level with video, and the type of presentation will all influence the direction.

Audio

Audio can be used as a standalone option, as part of the video, or even created by the participants, such as an exercise to write and sign a song.

Required Tools

For video with audio you will need some type of player, depending upon the media type:

- A DVD-ROM or Blu-ray player if you are using a video disc

- USB memory stick

- A laptop or PC with software to play digital video

You will also need a projector and a projection screen. Speakers are optional, but recommended for more than the smallest room and group.

Although today's cameras are light-sensitive, you may also need some simple lighting, such as a handyman light from a hardware store. If you want more than the onboard audio built into the camera, get a simple lavaliere or handheld microphone.

Finally, especially if budget is an issue, consider using one or more personal video devices -- such as smartphone. You'll also need a handful of inexpensive ear buds. You can pass the iPods around the room at certain times, or have participants up to view and listen to the material. While perhaps less formal than the others, this solution, is much more portable if your presentation is delivering off-site.

Tips and Tricks

Purchased Off-The-Shelf Video

- Check reviews of the media online

- Shop around for the best prices

- Preview the work before you purchase

- Test the video in conjunction with the exercise with a colleague before the presentation.

Personally created video

- Plan by creating a simple outline that matches your presentation content

- Create a storyboard using PowerPoint, a word processor, or paper before you record

- Check your equipment thoroughly

- Do a practice run before your final recording.

- Transfer the recording immediately to a computer for backup.

Professionally produced video from a production company

- Create an outline. (The storyboard may be provided by the production company.)

- Carefully create a request for proposal, and interview several companies

- Preview finished samples of each company's work

- Ask for a client list, and check with several of them

- Plan to dedicate an in-house resource person to work with the production company

- Manage costs through a preproduction meeting, trimming, if necessary, where it makes sense

- Maintain frequent two-way communication during the project

- If all proposals come in nearly equal, trust your instincts based on the relationships you have formed with the prospective companies

Creating a Plan B

Regardless of the method you use for your audio and video, it is essential to have a backup plan in the event that something goes awry with the technology.

- Have one or two backup copies of your media, perhaps on a USB flash drive and a DVD

- Test everything before the presentation

- For higher-end productions, have a technician on standby if possible

- Record and back up the audio track separately; if the video fails you will still have the audio

- Create a handout with the key concepts contained in your video

- Capture screen shots directly from the video (if permissible by copyright) and add them to a PowerPoint file

- If sequence isn't an issue, and you have access to a technician later, adjust your agenda to utilize the video later in the program.

If, for any reason, none of the above is feasible, consider substituting a role play between you and the selected participants. Above all, today's participants understand the "gotchas" when technology is involved, and will probably be empathetic as you carry on your presentation as if it was no big deal.

Chapter 10 – Pumping it Up a Notch

Bringing it to the next level is something you can accomplish after feeling comfortable with all of the previous topics discussed. You can add the little touches that will produce a lot of value during your presentation.

Make Them Laugh a Little

Humor is a popular way to liven up a presentation. It makes the audience align with you, and sends a signal that you are in charge. Handled properly, humor enriches a presentation.

When considering humor, make sure that whatever content you choose meets four criteria:

- You think the joke or lines are funny

- You can repeat the piece confidently and comfortably

- Your choice is not offensive to anyone (gender, race, age, disability, politics)

- Your audience will understand and appreciate what you are saying.

- A joke should have a punch line, delivered with all you've got.

Here are some tips for collecting and using humor:

- Jot down jokes as you hear them in everyday life; classify them as your collection grows

- Deliver any humor verbally only, and keep things light

- Match your humor to the demographics of the audience

- Research and consider using local humor if you're working off-site

- Don't be afraid to poke fun at yourself.

If a joke or delivering humor with words isn't within your comfort level, consider sharing a lighthearted cartoon, doing a simple magic trick, or doing something else that is unexpected and evokes a reaction and some emotion from the participants.

Ask Them a Question

Questions can be used in many ways, and at just about any time during your presentation.

- As an opener

- To check whether the desired learning is occurring, or to extend the learning experience

- To diffuse a difficult or uncomfortable situation

- To fill a long pause

- To get a feel about the mood in the room.

As we learned in module four, Verbal Communication Skills, you can use open, clarifying, or closed, questions, depending upon your needs.

Encouraging Discussion

Much of the discussion during your presentation will be structured to fit with the learning exercises. If a remark or question is made during a discussion that is off topic or something that should not be dealt with at the time, you can always add it to the parking lot, and return to it during the wrap-up to bring closure.

Dealing with Questions

Q&A Sessions: If time permits in your presentation, you may choose to hold a general question-and-answer session. Since as the presenter you are in control, you can decide when to stop the discussion. In a large room, be prepared to repeat each question. If no questions arise, be prepared to ask one yourself.

You can use an open question to begin the session: "What questions do you have?"

Restating Negative Questions: If a question is phrased negatively, restate it. For example, "Why have so many of his staff displayed chronic absenteeism?" can be restated as "Let's explore what we can do to reduce absenteeism in the team."

Off-topic: Don't forget about the parking lot if you receive an off-topic question.

Leveraging experience in the room: There may be situations when you wish to redirect a question to one of the participants. Again, you are in charge, so call upon someone and keep the discussion moving on afterward.

Additional Titles

The 90 Minute Guide series of books covers a variety of general business skills and are intended to be completed in 90 minutes or less. It is an effective way for building your skill set and can be used to acquire professional development units needed by project managers and other industries to maintain their certification. For the availability of titles please see https://www.silvercitypublications.com/shop/.

No. 1 - Appreciative Inquiry

No. 2 - Assertiveness and Self Control

No. 3 - Attention Management

No. 4 - Body Language Basics

No. 5 - Business Acumen

No. 6 - Business and Etiquette

No. 7 - Change Management

No. 8 - Coaching and Mentoring

No. 9 - Communications Strategies

No. 10 - Conflict Resolution

No. 11 - Creative Problem Solving

No. 12 - Delivering Constructive Criticism

No. 13 - Developing Creativity

No. 14 - Developing Emotional Intelligence

No. 15 - Developing Interpersonal Skills

No. 16 - Developing Social Intelligence

No. 17 - Employee Motivation

No. 18 - Facilitation Skills

No. 19 - Goal Setting and Getting Things Done

No. 20 - Knowledge Management Fundamentals

No. 21 - Leadership and Influence

No. 22 - Lean Process and Six Sigma Basics

No. 23 - Managing Anger

No. 24 - Meeting Management

No. 25 - Negotiation Skills

No. 26 - Networking Inside a Company

No. 27 - Networking Outside a Company

No. 28 - Office Politics for Managers

No. 29 - Organizational Skills

No. 30 - Performance Management

No. 31 - Presentation Skills

No. 32 - Public Speaking

No. 33 - Servant Leadership

No. 34 - Team Building for Management

No. 35 - Team Work and Team Building

No. 36 - Time Management

No. 37 - Top 10 Soft Skills You Need

No. 38 - Virtual Team Building and Management